Years by the Window

by

Selma Denmark

DORRANCE
PUBLISHING CO
EST. 1920
PITTSBURGH, PENNSYLVANIA 15238

Cover illustration by Helena Gomes Vaz
(Drawn by the author's granddaughter in 2020)

Translated by Tissiana F. Oliva

Original title:
ANOS DE JANELA

Editing of the original version, in Portuguese:
Wedja Leal, PhD

Dorrance Publishing Co
585 Alpha Drive
Pittsburgh, PA 15238
Visit our website at www.dorrancebookstore.com

ISBN: 978-1-6386-7327-9
eISBN: 978-1-6386-7355-2

FAREWELLS

What a sad thing to follow your silhouette
Fading away at a distance
Your features intertwined with those from the horizon
Your smell is now just a memory
Of your voice, I no longer have the source

But others surround you already
You get other hugs
Departures, arrivals,
My comfort is none, it is gone
May this instant live on without me

Poem by Rodrigo Vaz
(Composed by the author's son in 2016)

www.poesiaalguma.com.br

DEDICATION

To those who are disillusioned, frustrated, or unhappy on their path through life. I sincerely hope that after reading the following pages, written with the utmost simplicity and with all the candor these topics demand, you can understand this monumental truth: despite all the difficulties you may be facing, you should never lose sight that many of our brothers and sisters are wandering through life under much worse circumstances than us. So, be brave!

CONTENTS

Years by the Window

Throughout our existence, we get involved in numerous events of all sorts and different intensities. Certainly, we give rise to some of these situations ourselves; other times, they are brought about by other people, with whom we have shared our days and nights. Unfortunately, many such events leave aftereffects that weigh heavy in our hearts.

Anyone could certainly write about their own memories, recounting their past emotions, shattered dreams, and achievements.

Anyway, what I bring to you, dear reader, is a little bit of my own life experiences, as well as some from my invaluable journey companions, who have unknowingly served as inspiration to me, so as to diversify the subject matter.

The time spent recollecting the past has been a pleasurable one, because this is where only the joys and the events that have enriched our souls should be kept in our memories. And they shall remain there forever, even after we move on beyond this existence.

What I mean is the saddest and most devastating occurrences I have faced—the ones that have obstructed my pace but have been gradually overcome, though apparently unsurmountable at the time—those were tough to go over once again. Because I do not believe what is harmful should be preserved or remembered.

We must keep in mind that whatever happened in the past that was good is an invaluable treasure we carry along with us, and we must safeguard these memories in our hearts with all our love and affection.

I would like to clarify the title used so the reader does not think the name of the book is inaccurate. What does it mean, *Years by the Window*? If the book is based on real-life events and a wide range of true feelings and emotions, could it not be called *Years of Experience* or maybe *Years of Living*?

Yes, it could, but the expression in the title was passed on to me by someone very dear who is no longer among us. The expression has remained engraved in my mind and has never been erased from my memory. It is like a cherished keepsake of a loved one.

These pages will include a fraction of the many things I have already experienced, valuable adventures I am sharing in the hopes they may make a little difference in your precious existences, as a small and humble behavior model by which I have devised bit by bit my reason for living.

I do not claim or wish to come over as someone who has been able to reach a high level of perfection, wisdom, and understanding of the true meaning of what it is to live; on the contrary, I have merely figured out how to begin unraveling the tangled threads of life, and this means other challenges and new lessons will come; there will be more work to do within.

You see, my inner light finally kindled only after I had treaded a long path, as a reminder that it is always a good time to restart, to learn, and to renew oneself. One's age, in these cases, is irrelevant.

My first impetus was to put on paper some reflections about what we all carry in the archives of our memories; it pleased me to share my *Years by the Window* with friends.

I have then put together thirty texts or situations, whatever you wish to call them. These are the ones that have impressed me the most, and maybe you, my reader friend, will find some similarity with situations you have already experienced yourself. This will make me very happy, and I would be truly grateful for your personal comments if you wish to tell me something about any of these texts.

I have focused on writing about topics that are currently prominent, such as how the undesirable solitude can teach us that only time, this precious friend, can help us not to suffer the pain of existential emptiness.[1]

I have mentioned happiness and how hard it is nowadays to make sure we have a bit of this feeling to spice up our bitter days. I write about work, where our efforts in performing it must always be evident, so we can fulfill our duty with love and true responsibility, respecting our peers in our professional activities.

I bring up feelings of love, generosity, compassion, friendship, and hate; in sum, the ones that are most evident and have marked more intensely my journey through the years.

I sincerely hope my modest but genuine stories may entertain you; and if some of them remind you of a similar event, let us enjoy them together, while our minds and our hearts are still active.

Enjoy your reading!

Milton, New York, USA, July 17, 2020.
Selma Denmark
pazsel@hotmail.com

[1] According to psychologist Roberta Peripato, existential emptiness is present in the life of every single human being, to a greater or lesser degree. It is felt and experienced in several instances of the human existence. It emerges from peculiar and sometimes stressful situations in one's life. It can also be observed at times of grieving and losses experienced throughout a person's life. It permeates some psychological disorders and pathologies, such as depression itself. It is experienced, explicitly or implicitly, in the day-to-day of every human being each time the person wonders, reflects upon, or philosophizes on the real meaning of life. (2011)

1
HOPE

People say "While there is life, there is hope," but that is not always the case. Many people do not carry it in their hearts because they do not aim to achieve anything in life, nothing good, or even healthy. They just live their days, solely enjoying what they may offer, devoid of dreams, aspirations, or anything to hope for. They live as if they are carrying a heavy load over their shoulders.

To live without hope is to believe in nothing. But nothingness does not exist.

There will always be a higher power around that pushes us, though we do not notice it. A light that illuminates our steps, even if we do not see it. A blessing bestowed upon us, even if we do not feel it.

There is always something a lot greater than what our senses are capable of noticing; something sublime and unparalleled that we cannot even imagine due to our conceptual ignorance and moral deficit.

Yes, we must have hope for better days.

We must have hope that something new will happen to us and the moments of distress, depression, shortage, solitude, emptiness, and everything else shall pass.

During our existence, there will be many deserts to cross, which we devise ourselves because we are still incapable of choosing more accessible and dignified paths.

Despite all the difficulties that might emerge, these deserts are conquered bit by bit, because we are never forgotten or abandoned.

Unfortunately, we only realize that after many tears and a lot of pain and suffering.

Only then is hope born within us. And those who are able to raise it in their hearts shall never have to cross deserts or get caught up by inertia again.

Thus, to feed the flames of hope that lie within our inner self in a dormant state is to ensure that, with the dawn of a new day, we shall find an oasis of solace.

And, who knows, maybe a new, fresh start awaits us—with fewer challenges, more serenity and safety—in a near, better future.

Tomorrow will be another day, and everything will be all right!

2
FORGIVENESS

Someone offends, hurts, upsets, or slanders us. What will our reaction be? How can we possibly not react at all and even forget an injustice done upon us if, most of the time, we are innocent victims who have done nothing to deserve this?

Did we indeed do nothing to deserve it?

If we go over the unpleasant event once again, could there be something we can attribute to ourselves as the reason for the misunderstanding?

Maybe a small gesture, or even a less than courteous word that may have escaped from us, may have created a conflict.

It is very difficult to forget and forgive... thus so many people say: "I will never forgive" or even "I will never forget."

If we remain in this wavelength of resentment and outrage, we will drag ourselves to a mental state of shadows that will hinder our moral evolution. And it will certainly cause serious problems to our physical body too.

If someone hurts us, even if it is unfair, we must do everything we can to redirect our thoughts so we do not put ourselves at the same level as the person who has offended us. We often must also act as if we are deaf. Under the circumstances, this is the wise thing to do.

As much as it may hurt, if we really did not deserve the offense, then the problem is not ours; it pertains to the person who has offended us.

By acting in this manner, we promptly initiate a forgiveness process, without even realizing it.

Maybe the person who has offended or hurt us is struggling with conflicts within and is in a moral state that is slightly opposed to ours—who knows.

When we forgive someone, something within us ascends; we become lighter, more secure and confident because we realize we have done the right thing; because a mere slander will not be enough to make us lose our emotional control. It is not worth it.

As the days go by, the pain, the outrage, the desire never to forget what has happened become less important; it does not hurt as much anymore because we understand we should never fight against disturbed minds.

We must keep in mind that those who have hurt us are also here to learn how to respect each person's limits, given we are all brothers and sisters. We do not all learn our lessons at the same time, though.

We shall then reach the following conclusion: we must forgive those who have hurt us so we may also be forgiven for the mistakes we make every day.

Are we not all constantly evolving souls just passing through this existence?

Well, the past no longer belongs to us, then. And that is no place to stay. To forget, maybe never; but to forgive, always.

3
SUFFERING

Every time we are affected by suffering, we promptly wonder, Why is this happening to me? Instead, the question should be, Where did I make a mistake?

We must go over past events that have affected us and look for their initial cause; for what it is we did or did not do so these events ended up reaching such proportions. Or even for what we heedlessly did that gave rise to our suffering.

We will then realize we are in control of our own misfortunes. We should not blame anyone, not even the Divine Providence, like most people do.

To acknowledge we are responsible for the troubles that affect us and must not find fault with anyone constitutes maturity in a moral sense; it reflects interior growth.

If we make a mistake, we fall and suffer; let us pick up the broken pieces, let us get back up from our own pain and start over.

The sun rises every day, bringing us refreshing mornings.

If today it feels almost impossible to keep going, if we reach "rock bottom," as they say, let us think: Within every living being, there is a strength we do not yet fully comprehend, but it pushes us, constantly. Let us not ignore it.

We cannot and must not give up, ever. We need to keep in mind that we are apprentice souls, still quite imperfect, searching for our enlightenment.

We are here on this planet of suffering and challenges in order to learn something that maybe we have not figured out yet; we are on our way there, though.

When we trip and fall, we will get up and start again and again, no matter how many times it takes.

The pain always comes to teach us we need to recognize we have made mistakes and something must be repaired.

If we lack the strength, let us remember the "footprints in the sand"[2] and keep going...

---

[2] "Footprints in the Sand" Poem: [...] Lord, you said that once I decided to follow you, you would walk with me all the way; but I have noticed that during the most troublesome times in my life, there is only one set of footprints. I do not understand why in times when I needed you the most, you should leave me. The Lord replied, "My precious, precious child. I love you, and I would never, ever leave you during your times of trial and suffering. When you saw only one set of footprints, it was then that I carried you."

4
RENOVATION

The years go by, and everything we were and did stays behind.

In nature, everything is transformed and starts anew. We, human beings, are always starting a new stage of our lives as well.

Yes, we must renovate constantly; we must be better today than we were yesterday. After all, is that not what we have come here to do?

We must always evolve, get rid of bad habits and vices, arrogance, envy, jealousness, selfishness, and hate; these feelings impoverish our souls and hinder our journey on this planet Earth, where pain and suffering still prevail.

Many people claim they would not change a thing about themselves for anyone, not even for themselves. So many of us have already heard something like this, even from beloved relatives. These words demonstrate such poverty of soul; these creatures still have so much to live, to walk, to learn and progress.

Life is constantly starting over and the paths we have already treaded, which have led us to endless precipices, will not be stepped on again, especially not by those who really wish to reach what is beyond the horizon—because they can use our directions and lessons as a compass.

Our greatest challenge is to leave behind our mistakes, vices, weaknesses, and pettiness in order to win over ourselves.

We are like raw stones that need to be polished, bit by bit, to allow our inner light to shine on.

If we look towards the past as we get rid of the darkness we have been involved in due to misuse of our free will,[3] we will realize we are no longer the same people we were before; we are no longer a dull rock or a creature that creeps aimlessly.

It is so good to know our existence has not been in vain; that we have been turning into better human beings, cultivating noble feelings that make us more lenient towards others' imperfections; that we are making the effort, every day, to change our habits, our way of thinking and living.

Getting rid of our immaturity and spiritual ignorance, cultivating more edifying virtues and qualities.

Walking side by side with our brothers and sisters, which we all are, exchanging values acquired through this long journey of life.

We must, therefore, constantly renovate our inner self so tomorrow we can be better than we are today.

This is what the Lord of life really expects from us.

---

[3] Free will is the power each person has to choose their actions, which path to take. The expression is used in several religions, such as Christianism, Spiritism, Buddhism, etc. The real meaning of free will has religious, psychological, moral, and scientific connotations. For some people, free will means to have freedom—and many people mistake this with disrespect and bad manners. Everyone really does have the right to do as they wish, as long as they do not cause harm to anyone else. (www.significados.com.br)

5
FAITH

How can such a small word contain such strength? With faith, one can move mountains of sorrows that form all around us. In what stage of life does it manifest in us, such sacred feeling that connects us directly to the Creator?

During childhood, we do not yet know what it is to have faith; but it does manifest itself in a subtle way, in our innermost being.

Because, while we are kids, we entrust our tranquility and confidence to those around us, those who support and affectionately care for us—our parents, grandparents, uncles, aunts, and godparents, in other words, those in charge of our protection, livelihood, and development.

In our youth, we no longer require so much protection and vigilance, but faith is still far from manifest in us, because life during adolescence is an ocean of novelties and nothing concerns us.

We believe in our own ability to choose. We know—or rather we think we know—what we want and where we are heading. Our choices are always right and any advice people try to give us is not worthwhile or heeded.

But when we finally reach maturity, when the nights are so long that dawn seems to be miles away, when our strength dwindles and the weight we carry from our pains and disappointments are unbearable, who must we beseech?

Only then do we realize there is an incalculable strength within us, a strong feeling that supports and encourages us to continue our journey.

We then realize that, as hard as things may be, we are certainly not alone; relief will come, and peace shall reign in our hearts.

We reach this sublime moment in our lives when faith manifests itself and grows within us into a robust faith, one that does not lose balance before any emotional or moral disorder.

When we finally learn to feed our faith with perseverance and abnegation, we must be grateful because we shall then be able to have peace and spiritual serenity.

We must have faith in our tomorrow, in the days to come; we must have confidence in our ability to know when it is time to wait; and we must accept whatever happens to us because we understand everything that is meant for us and everything we need shall somehow be provided to us.

But it shall be provided to us at the right time, not whenever we want or demand it.

This is what it means to have faith. This certainty nurtures our souls, warms our hearts, and eases our minds.

It involves us in a light, which we need in order to better identify the right paths to take from then on.

6
LOVE

Oh, how I love you!

How many times have we said that? How many times has love touched our hearts and enriched our lives?

What is love if not the greatest of all virtues, which has been passed on to us since the early stages of our lives and eventually started growing within our hearts as time went by?

What is this feeling that makes us thrill with delight for our significant other, loved ones, pets, objects, and things?

Love is so diverse and its power so intense it may even disarm a fierce enemy when given in return for the hate directed at us.

Oh, love! A sweet feeling that makes us look at life with such happiness that, when it suddenly comes, we no longer see problems around us. Everything else is relative.

Love, by itself, is enough to enrich our existences. Who can say they have never experienced such love—so unexpected and so powerful?

Oh, it is so good to love, in the broad sense of the term, without expecting anything in return, not even special consideration. Without any demands. Simply to love, unconditionally.

This is what true love is. This is what has been given to us originally and what makes us noble and great before the world.

Because the bliss of loving in this way is so precious that the more love we give, the more this sublime feeling overflows in our hearts.

Those who have suffered a lot tend to love very intensely because they have managed, as the years went by, to add this sweet and invaluable feeling that is love to life's adversities.

To love, always; to love, eternally...

Because love builds, reinforces, strengthens. Love rescues, forgives, and assists.

Love overcomes the barriers of moral ignorance and improves us each step of the way towards happiness, which is reserved for us.

So, let us love ourselves first and then spread this love to those who walk by our side; this powerful feeling that turns us into righteous creatures before our immortality...

7
DEATH

Who has never experienced the pain of losing a loved one? Who does not still weep for the absence of those who have been, in life, the reason for our existence?

How can we find comfort for such a significant loss? How can we accept such a tragedy that has struck us and continues to slowly wear us down? Who can we resort to for comfort and understanding?

What is the point of being here, most of the time facing constant pain and suffering, and then leave?

And who shall meet us when we arrive there? That is, if "there" exists indeed. But who can assure us, with the utmost certainty, that there is nothing "there"?

How can we find comfort to such strong pain and devastating void left by those who have left, leaving us with no strength to keep going, with our lives shattered?

Only after death has paid a visit, taking away from us someone who had been our sole reason to live, only then do we ask ourselves what to believe in.

Could there possibly be nothing? Could this be the end of everything for our loved ones who have left? And how about ourselves, who have stayed behind... how can we go on?

It has been said—and science has confirmed—that there are more stars in the firmament than grains of sand in all the deserts on Earth. In this case, what could there be in the sky that our pettiness still cannot reach?

There is a whole vastness we cannot even begin to understand yet, maybe because we lack sharper and more advanced senses that would allow us to comprehend it.

If there is a supreme power conducting this endless immensity, what would be the reasoning for birth, growth, death?

We must therefore await, with patience and resignation, embracing our sorrows with courage and confidence in our tomorrow.

If there is something superior, beyond our psychological, moral, and spiritual ignorance, if there is a higher Conductor in command of this infinite universal orchestra, let us not lose heart even though we have not yet figured out our purpose.

If we have confidence in this love Conductor, we shall have the necessary strength to bear the pain caused by this void, by the absence of our loved ones.

Let us wait, because today's pain shall be superseded by the overwhelming joy of being reunited with those who have preceded us in this trip to beyond the horizon.

To believe is to live in peace and to accept the immense void, to know there is an explanation for everything. The unknown is still unfathomable to us, though.

Let us keep in mind that when we keep those who have gone in our hearts, there is no absence, because they are very close.

8
CHRISTMAS

He always comes when our strength, hope, and faith have dwindled and we are overthrown by the weight of our bad choices and decisions, as if struck by a storm that destroys everything on its path.

Feeling defeated, we end up destroying all the purest emotions we have inside, which He has given us long ago. We then feel sorry for ourselves.

Actually, He does not come, because He never leaves. He is always by our side, just waiting for our call, because He does not interfere with our free will. He waits until we are tired of making mistake, after mistake, completely misled...

It is unfortunate that we never notice His presence in our lives, we never feel His unparalleled energy involving us with such kindness and so much love!

We are still insensitive to the most noble emotions that lift us up and instead focus only on those that bring us closer to our irrational instincts.

We should not remember or think of Him solely on this date when we celebrate Christmas, when we finally pause our daily rush, with its hectic pace, to gather with family and exchange gifts, before a table laden with delicacies prepared with love to celebrate His birth.

Most of us, though, do not realize that Christmas is His party. It is for Him.

Humankind, wake up! There is still time. Let us allow Him to be born within our homes. Not just on Christmas Day, but every day.

Let us not allow our hearts to harden as to the needs of those around us.

Let us help those who have fallen along the way to get back up and those who are lagging behind to reach us.

Let us look at those who have hurt or upset us—often times when we have not even done anything to provoke them—and think: their souls are ill and they need compassion.

Let us interact with those people from our family circle who are still mistaken and may even have abandoned us because they have gotten themselves tangled in the thorn bush of pride, vanity, and selfishness.

Let us cultivate in our minds only good thoughts. Whenever a bad thought attempts to take over, and its shadows attempt to dominate us, let us raise our thoughts to the Creator of this vast universe, He who has mercy on us for our weaknesses and compassion for our ignorance, which is still immense. He, the supreme sovereign, who always gives us a new opportunity.

This is the real meaning of Christmas festivities, to thank the One whose birthday is being celebrated for the blessings bestowed upon us, from the bottom of our hearts. Even if we still cannot feel His presence beside us, or even if we do not have faith, or have a different belief, the truth is, He never abandons us.

He said it Himself: "All the sheep that my Father has entrusted to me, none will be lost."

To celebrate Christmas is to notice Jesus, always so close.

To let Him be part of our daily lives.

To walk alongside our Master and allow ourselves to get involved by His peace, which is not the same as the one the world may offer us, because the peace of Jesus brings us closer to one another "fraternally."

9
HAPPINESS

How can we achieve happiness in our lives when most of our days and nights are spent among so many sorrows, disappointments, and regrets?

How can we overcome so many hardships and allow the joy of living to reach us, thus lightening the load of misfortunes that pile up all around us?

What can we do, then, to achieve happiness? We realize we are still quite morally imperfect and have a lot more to learn about ourselves. That is why we are constantly amid whirlwinds of hurdles that we generate ourselves.

Yes, the woes in which we always find ourselves in, we create ourselves; are we not the ones in the driver's seat through the paths of life?

Everything that happens to us, then, whether we want it or not, is the result of our own heedless attitudes—whether recent ones or maybe actions from our past.

And what is happiness or moments of joy when our monetary savings are so scarce; when opportunities of a better job, which would help us succeed, do not materialize for us; when we feel completely powerless?

Happiness is the certainty that we are doing what is right and fair even as we face all the hurdles that show up in our path; that we are always acting in good faith towards everyone who shares our existence.

We achieve peace when we get to the end of each day and, after analyzing our own attitudes, come to realize we have left behind a small trail of good conduct, of accomplished duty. A sign we have tried to do our part in the best possible way so that our righteous attitudes may be followed as a humble role model for those who are trailing along with us in this journey of life.

The peace of knowing that, at the end of the day, we are a little bit better than we were the day before, fulfilling the obligations our job demands with satisfaction.

All of this within our limitations, of course. Even if every single thing is not perfect; even if we still have obstacles to overcome and emotional imbalances to adjust due to our inner flaws.

Even if we are presented with difficult decisions to make in the future, simply knowing we are on the right path, doing what is right, having our conscience as our guide, is that not happiness? Even if it is relative, fleeting...

So, let us enjoy it while it lasts, because my experience tells me that, after a wave of joy, there is always another one of deep sorrow.

This happiness we experience from time to time is enough to reinvigorate our strength and our courage to keep going.

We know that complete joy is not yet possible because, aside from our own human weaknesses, we still need to deal with our loved ones, friends, fellow workers, and travel companions. And we do not always vibrate in the same frequency, so it is often hard to maintain these relationships well balanced.

We are constantly bombarded by slander, intrigues, and all sorts of "nitpicking." These are all major challenges we must overcome wisely. This certainly does disturb our emotional tranquility and brings a bitter taste to our existence.

Happiness, then, is knowing how to cherish the precious moments life gives us every once in a while. It also means knowing how to preserve them in our memory forever...

Who can say they have never experienced a moment of joy?

We must, therefore, store within us the joy of those happy moments we have experienced, as a sacred supply that shall hold us together when happiness, once again, eludes us.

10
PLEA

After treading steep slopes that took me nowhere; after forgetting the sublime teachings that used to nurture my heart, here I am, with all the humility I have inherited from You, to lift my thoughts up to the highest heights in an attempt to reach You with a humble plea.

Even though You know what is in my heart, I tear it all apart and make my plea—that You may allow me to go through this door that has been opened to me. With everything that is alive in me, I beg You.

You are always following my footsteps and frequently; when it becomes difficult or even impossible for me to continue on my path, You extend me Your helping hand and encourage me not to give up, because You know me better than I know myself.

I know I am still a diamond in the rough and I have done very little so far to turn into one of the precious jewels in Your valuable treasure. But I am walking towards this goal, even if my pace is slow and though I may sometimes stumble.

There is no use living in this island of uncertainties, surrounded by unyielding, indifferent beings who do not care for those who are creeping in the depths of incomprehension and despair.

I want larger horizons; I want to reach the top of the hill with my own two feet, without offending or even running over anyone around me.

I want it, because You have given me this right when I arrived here.

So hear me, Master of the masters, give me the opportunity to continue in this new path that has opened up before me and filled me with new hope.

Allow me to search for better pastures for my small herd. Allow me to achieve my highest goal and enrich me with strength and wisdom so I can carve out my place in the sun.

If You so wish, though, I shall continue my daily struggle in this endless despair; I only ask that You strengthen me with Your unconditional love and involve me in Your comforting peace so I may never complain about my sorrows and limitations.

And then I shall never wrongfully accuse You of having abandoned me.

11
VICE

Willingly or otherwise, a vice is a physical dependence that causes great damage to one's health and is very hard to be tackled. It is a great evil that we feed daily, sometimes without even realizing it; and this starts to enslave us little by little.

Because we are all evolving beings amid constant internal conflicts, we get attached to certain habits as an "escape valve" in order to face the difficult situations we encounter ahead of us. Often times, these habits throw us totally off balance.

We do not realize this vice drags us through life, leaving us unable to take control of the situation.

We always say we can stop this harmful vice whenever we want and deem convenient, but it is not that easy.

People around us often point out that we keep repeating an attitude, gesture, or even words constantly without realizing it; likewise, we do not have the strength to stop this because it has already become a habit.

This is especially the case for more serious vices such as tobacco, alcohol, drugs, gambling, and so many others, which cause grave emotional distress and severe dependence that is so hard to overcome.

The vice always ends up hurting us and especially those who love us. Most of the time, however, our attitude is to ignore the advice from our loved ones who only wish to see us free from our vice—which is, unfortunately, already ingrained.

Whatever our vice is, it is good to know we will certainly need help to get rid of it.

We need, therefore, to be self-motivated—sometimes extraordinarily so—and to have great willpower if we are to stop doing something that gives us false pleasure and is slowly harming us. We tend to ignore or even contradict this truth, though.

An immense sadness invades our hearts when we see someone, especially from our family circle or our friends' group, creeping along cumbersomely through life, hauling some sort of vice, and there is no possible way we can help.

That is because we know the consequences shall be great sorrow for these creatures, who are crushing themselves in a slow self-destruction process, a sort of indirect suicide, because of this vice they cannot get rid of. And they often do not even realize it.

Whatever the vice is, it is always harmful to the body and soul's health. To overcome this evil that has taken over us for so long, we will need to want help in the first place. Otherwise, nobody will be able to assist us.

Then, we must take over total control of the situation. In order to do that, we rely on the help of qualified professionals, true friends, and especially our loved ones.

It is not impossible, though we must say it sure is challenging. Thus, we must love ourselves in the first place. We must boost our self-esteem and nurture respect for the life that has been bestowed upon us, because one day we shall be accountable for everything we have done while alive.

We also want our bodies to enjoy good health up until the time comes for us to leave this existence, having in our conscience the satisfaction of knowing we have at least tried to do what was best for ourselves.

Help always comes; we only need to "want" it.

12
SOLITUDE

Oh, dear Solitude, my inseparable companion; my friend, nowadays. You involve me in tenderness and solace.

A long time ago, you filled my days with sadness and agony. In those days, I cried out to the four winds for someone who had struck my heart with an unparalleled love. And you, my friend Solitude, hijacked the hours and tortured my existence.

You have made me shed so many tears, you have involved my soul—tired of always being lonely amongst the crowd—in so much pain and sorrow.

Oh, dear Solitude, in those times I crept through life and did not live; those were barren, dry deserts I have crossed without realizing I existed.

I also did not realize at the time that you, my friend Solitude, kept on carefully pushing me forward. Because even you could see my despair and shared with me the uncertainties of a hopeless future, deprived of a reason to be hopeful—a future filled with much loneliness.

But the cure always comes: TIME. This dear friend has supported us and gradually made us even closer. And we started understanding each other, getting to know each other.

You were no longer a cruel enemy; I had gotten used to having you by my side. I had finally learnt to live with you, through days and nights.

I started opening up and sharing my most intimate secrets with you, turning you into my comforting friend, my private wall for my deepest wailings.

I would share with you my constantly escalating uncertainties. I started to seek in you the antidote for my deepest and most intimate evils.

Then, as time—this long-standing dear friend—went by, you became part of my existence, not as a cruel enemy but as an ally that held me up in the hours of exhaustion and in the respites from the daily rush.

You, my dear Solitude, then started to stay by my side at all times. But you no longer filled me with pain and sorrow; you nurtured my soul. You motivated me in the search for my greater self and helped me to finally understand there was something great within the most intimate part of my being. You have also taught me to allow the most beautiful, dormant parts of me to flow freely.

I then started realizing it was necessary for me to meet you, Solitude. Because only then did I understand what life expected from me.

I was only able to find this long-lost treasure of great beauty within me after you hurt and drew blood from me.

Today, dear Solitude, we understand each other like soul mates.

You fill in the voids that still need to be explored, and I turn you into my companion, my ally, and my educator, dear Solitude!

13
ENVY

What is this feeling that makes us bitter when something good happens to someone around us?

A weird feeling that diminishes us before others and makes us run away to avoid witnessing someone else's joy—because, as far as we know, we should be the privileged ones, the distinguished ones.

What is this feeling? And how can we hide the frustration we feel in these situations? How can we display joy for something good that is happening to others and not to us? When we are not the center of attentions?

How can we be happy for someone else's joy and share feelings we have not yet cultivated?

What is this feeling of craving what others have, coveting the extraordinary things that happen to them, and longing for the happy moments others enjoy while we are stuck with misfortunes and limitations?

What is this feeling we attempt to hide, displaying a fake semblance to disguise what lies deep within us? Displaying sympathy when, in reality, we are outraged and our pride is hurt, both of which we have not yet figured out.

It is the capital sin called envy. It is an evil that invades humankind's minds and hearts because we still walk in the shadows of ignorance and the unknown.

An envious person easily forgets the blessings we receive every day. Is our heart not still beating? How about the blessing of life? This is probably one of the blessings we often forget. How can we get rid of this evil, then?

We should begin by learning to be content with what we have, who we are, and what we have already accomplished. Then we should look around and realize that, if today we want more, we have that right too, like everyone else.

When we no longer value what other people have and all they continue to get as much, then we will begin to value what is ours, even if it is not much.

We will then have won a small internal battle and that shall bring us a bit of emotional tranquility, which we have not yet experienced.

Gradually, we will work on our wounded self-esteem, changing our ways of thinking and acting.

We will also repeat to ourselves, in the privacy of our personal retreat, that everything that happens to us is because we needed it. Also, even if we cannot comprehend it at the moment, this is what we have to work on; therefore, we must keep going.

After all, who would be able to provide us with tomorrow's reports?

We do know, however, that tomorrow will be the result of what we are currently cultivating and building within and around us.

14
GUILT

Our existence is like a long road, full of unexpected pitfalls, crossroads, and surprises. But it is not just boulders and thorns; we also pass by beautiful landscapes, where we can pause to simply admire it or even to recover from the hike.

Throughout this long journey of life, we often take some shortcuts. In other words, we make some wrong decisions, which later bring us regret.

That is when guilt comes along. It brings us so much sorrow to realize we would not have such a guilty conscience today if we had done things differently or chosen different paths.

Given we cannot change the past, what can we do to fix a mistake and stop mulling over the harm we have done, often inadvertently? Well, we cannot change what has been done; we do not have this power.

We can, of course, ask for forgiveness. However, even if we are forgiven, the guilt will linger inside of us; the effects of our mistake will remain with us as a memory, hurting our souls with remorse and regret.

We end up feeding this guilt inside of us for a long time, instead of enjoying the present moment. We fixate on the past we should have left behind, which will not come back. What should we do, then?

We must recognize we have made a mistake and, above all, forgive ourselves. We must get rid of this guilt. After all, are we not all still apprentices of the way? We have not been told which way we should go. We use our free will as a compass.

Next, we must remediate our mistake by doing some good; it does not matter what or to whom. What really matters is to keep moving forward, helping our trail companions along.

Finally, we must also work on our feelings and emotions in order to establish an inner peace. Even though we know we have made a mistake, we must not condemn ourselves forever.

Opportunities to be of service abound and so does our ability to help. In fact, we may do much good to someone who is completely disillusioned by their fellow human beings merely by offering a sincere smile.

There is always something we can do. We will then start to feel the weight of this guilt we carry gradually lighten up.

There is really no way of undoing what has been done. But we can learn from our mistakes, control our unruly impulses, and make careful and wise decisions from then on.

We can also heal the wound by helping those we have harmed, if they will let us. If this opportunity is not extended to us, we can point our solidarity to a different direction.

This positive attitude will certainly lighten the weight of the guilt we may carry.

15
CHILDREN

Our children are gifts from heaven, the most precious gift a human being can get. Each child with their own personality, their own story to tell, their own path to follow, and their own book of life yet to be written.

Our children are rare jewels, but they do not belong to us.

Instead, they are valuable loans—though we cannot constantly hide away from the world for fear they will be stolen from us. Likewise, we cannot have them simply to adorn our existences. We must guide them towards the right path, towards immortality.

We must fill in the first pages of their personal stories with wise guidance to make them strong enough to bear any storm that may eventually develop on their path.

Our children spend a small part of their lives by our side, but most of us do not appreciate the real value of this unforgettable time together, which should be solely dedicated to their guidance, to stimulating their gifts, and to staving off their premature vices.

Yes, they are our children, but only while they are still young and defenseless. As soon as they become adults, they leave on a one-way trip to fulfill the cycle of life, in an unrelenting search for adventures and dreams to be conquered.

The days and nights past, filled with moments of innocent bliss spent together when they were still young, remain engraved in our memories to enrich our souls once we reach maturity.

The memories of these past golden and unforgettable moments fill us with "pride and contentment."

Our children do not belong to us, though. They belong to life.

And life shall hold us accountable for what we have made of them, for how many seeds of good principles and dignity we have sprouted in their immortal souls, thus helping them become good people.

Yes, it is true; they do not belong to us, and we do not have the right to treat them like our private property. Because nothing belongs to us.

We have come here with nothing, and we shall leave with nothing...

As parents, we must devote our love and dedication, our affection and respect, our wisdom and insight to our children—and not merely because this is a law of nature, but because it is our duty.

That is how it is; we have come before them so we could teach them the way!

16
LONGING

Time goes by and the distance increases; the longing suffocates me, and I cannot hold back the tears...

Life follows its course; the days are filled with commitments that cannot wait; thus, there is not much time for the pain of longing to escalate.

Weeks, months, years fly away quickly, but my routine is always the same. Hectic days filled with so many tasks and nights when exhaustion prevents me from crying because of this longing that now lives within me.

Nights when dreams await us—because, from now on, that is where we meet, once in a while.

In my dreams... that is where you show up, always smiling, and talk to me. The tenderness of your voice echoes in my ears day after day, like an angelical melody of extraordinary beauty.

I have watched you grow, realized your aspirations, and appreciated your budding talents—which were many—from an early age. I was sure you would thrive regardless which one of those talents you decided to dedicate yourself to.

I had imagined you among the chosen ones on Earth. Maybe that was pretentious, but I had anticipated a successful future for you, filled with great accomplishments.

You were always a leader among the little ones, who loved you very much. Because you were the one who maintained balance and harmony among them.

Whenever possible, we were always together. Visiting the little ones, eating out, going shopping—even though I knew you did not enjoy it, I always took you along with me.

In your usual humility, you always repeated you did not need anything. You always said everything was fine and what you really wanted was to be with the ones who were part of your existence whenever possible or to engage in one of your precious gifts.

Sometimes we talked about small secrets, about dreams, or about something funny. Your smile, still present in my memory, was innocent and contagious.

When we were all together, there was only joy; it was always one big party.

It has been a few years spent together, which shall never get lost in time or in eternity. The memory of you is present in everyone who knew you. You are still very close.

We never imagined this precious time would be so little, though. We never thought the unfortunate fate would yank you away from us. We could not fathom it would rattle your thoughts and take you away, so we could no longer be with you. The pain caused by this loss was so great; it was immeasurable.

I have stopped fighting for my right to be with you for at least a few days once in a while. I have stopped and allowed time itself to show you the most important thing is your happiness, your wellbeing, and your brilliant future.

I have stopped, but I did not forget you. I do not ever forget you and I never will, for as long as I exist, for as long as there is life in me. And life is immortality.

Today, I do not know if you are happy; I do not know if you are living your most precious dreams; I do not know what has become of you.

Regardless of what may happen, or how long it may take, I will be waiting for you; I will wait… We shall be reunited someday.

Meanwhile, I will be carrying you in my heart, wishing you the best always, and telling you, like I always did:

"I love you to infinity and beyond."

17
COMPASSION

I feel sorry for you if you walk through dark pathways, dodging the light so as not to transpire all the inequity that dwells in your heart without you even realizing it.

If you allow your self-esteem to speak louder, thus ignoring the limits of your freedom to act—where it begins and where it ends—I feel very sorry for you.

I also feel sorry for you if you are interfering in the destiny of those entrusted to you, altering the events in your favor, focusing solely on yourself in order to reach your petty and selfish goals.

If right now you have no peace and find yourself engaged in skewed battles that are slowly destroying the most beautiful ideals of those around you, and if there is nothing that can possibly be done to pause this unhinged rat race in which you do not live the present moment, being completely fixated on the endless pursuit to achieve your goals, suffering and causing pain to those who love you, I sympathize with you.

Finally, if you prefer to isolate yourself in your inner solitude, cultivating perverse emotions such as hate, outrage, and the desire for revenge—which are like destructive poisons for the body and soul—then I feel immense compassion for you.

There are noble qualities in you, because your essence is divine. But you no longer cultivate them, because materialism has vitiated your mind and dried up your heart.

I am no longer part of your life; I know nothing about your days and nights. There is nothing I can do to rescue you, because you do need help, but you have not realized it yet.

We are distant, like the sun in relation to the moon. And there is a great abyss between us. I see you falling into this abyss. Unfortunately, your fall—and your pain—will be considerable...

I wish I could alert you of what awaits you and tell you about what can still be done. We are so puny and ignorant; we make mistakes and unheeded decisions. We can always start all over again, though.

Is life not, incidentally, one big school? Are we not all elementary students? And does our Master not give us endless opportunities to reconsider our mistakes so we can finally get it right in our next attempt?

But you are boundlessly stubborn; you always want to be right, because you have not yet comprehended the purpose of our existence and what must be the crucial point of our battle, which is to live. You have also not yet realized we shall be accountable for our actions at the end of this existence, in other words, all the good we have cultivated and spread out.

You are wasting precious time from your short existence. The future comes very swiftly, and along with it comes the final reckoning.

You will then face pain and tears, the remorse for having caused sorrow in so many hearts will bring you extraordinary distress.

I have immense compassion for you, because you have chosen to take the path of sorrow, of darkness.

But do not ever forget that I am here and that I will always be waiting with open arms whenever you wish to return.

"Love overcomes a multitude of mistakes."

18
DOUBT

There are moments, along our walk through the paths of life, in which we face a crossroad. Then, we ask ourselves, What should we do?

There is absolutely no possibility of backtracking, because the days must continue their course towards infinity. And we cannot stay put either; we are forced to move forward.

Which way should we go, though, if there are no signs to indicate the way or guide us when we must make a choice?

Most of the time, many of us do not realize the path we choose to take shall lead us to our summit or to our failure. Therefore, we do not give it as much thought as this moment requires.

Our ability to choose is still very unstructured, because we are so slow to learn the secrets and mysteries imposed on us by our existence, so we simply take whichever path appears to be the best one to us.

Oh, if only we could possibly take a sneak peek into all these different paths, into all these opportunities that arise in front of us, to see what awaits us at the end of each one of them. That would make a huge difference in our existence; we would get it right every time.

We would certainly always choose the path that would offer us an easier access, that would bring us only joy. We would then follow along a colorful path, filled with pleasures, and we would not have to make any effort at all. There would be no struggles, challenges, or devastating adversities.

As we approached the end and looked back, though, we would realize our existence had been empty and totally meaningless.

We would not end up with the satisfaction of knowing our mission had been accomplished, because nothing of value or inspiring had been built by ourselves.

Everything that had happened would have been attributable to an existence free of obstacles, pain, and suffering, where inertia was our companion. Thus, there would be no merit to enrich our souls and lift us up above life, beyond life.

We would have been like soldiers who had remained in the background and had never actually confronted the enemy, so likewise there would be no badges of honor for us.

Yes, the mountains of sorrow, the insidious blows from those who have shared our journey, the disappointments, and the emotional imbalances that constantly strike us are precious teachings that life gives us, and these are the enlightening lessons we need for our inner enrichment.

It really does seem like it is an ironic fate, that we need a whole life, filled with so many challenges, turbulences, and dreadful events, to grasp what our stubbornness prevents us from learning.

Oh, how puny and ignorant we are regarding good living!

On the other hand, not having anyone to point us towards the right path to follow, most of the time we simply take whatever direction and go ahead.

Gradually, we start to realize that it will not be easy, that we will be facing many storms and crossing huge deserts due to our incoherent choices.

As unexperienced travelers that we all are, just passing through life, we are always juggling material needs and the lack of more accessible opportunities.

Doubt is always present in any situation throughout our existence because we are still far from mastering everything we need to learn.

We make unheeded decisions; we follow our instincts; we let ourselves be led by someone else's opinions; and sometimes we even test our luck—all in an attempt to find the right direction to go.

Doubt schlepps us from side to side and we are constantly dangling between right and wrong.

The important thing, though, is not to let the feeling of failure get to us when we eventually realize we have made more mistakes than wise decisions.

As bad as it may have been, we must accept it because we have acted to the best of our knowledge at that time. We did not know any better then. Maybe if these past events had happened today, we would act differently—who knows?

This is the acknowledgement that we are evolving, learning with the obstacles we gradually face and eliminate throughout our existence.

This is the realization that we will certainly continue to make mistakes, because we are still in the infancy of our wisdom, but they will not be the same mistakes we had made before.

From now on, if any doubt emerges again, we must use our common sense, which by now has been enriched by precious lessons we have received and developed along the way.

Yes? No? Quite the opposite: YES! NO!

19
GENEROSITY

Generosity is one of the virtues we must necessarily cultivate throughout our passage, through the millennia ahead of us.

People who are generous, who give much of themselves without expecting anything in return, even if they do not follow a specific religion; those who are always ready to offer help, to assist the needy whenever possible; those people are among the blessed ones on planet Earth.

Many of them do not even imagine how many blessings reach heaven every single day in exchange for the good deeds received by those humble creatures who can recognize and acknowledge the kindness of their benefactors.

It is so good to know there are still people who care about their journey companions and the less fortunate.

When we give something away, regardless of what it is—a piece of advice at a moment of doubt, a compliment that may be able to lift up someone's self-esteem, a favor done with some urgency, or even some financial assistance—the satisfaction of being able to be of service, of donating something of ours, is priceless.

The joy that emanates from the person who has been the beneficiary of our good deed, which is the reflection of the gratitude they feel, is enough for us—because there is nothing as valuable as this.

This is especially the case when nothing is requested from us, when we give something away because we realize the need, without having to be asked.

But when we are the ones in need of assistance, what should we do and who should we ask for help?

In these instances, we tend to look among our friends and relatives for someone who might be able to alleviate the weight of our responsibilities. What an unwelcome surprise it is when we hear no in response!

Oh, such anguish and disappointment! A feeling of rage mixed with humiliation takes over us, because our dignity is left exposed to unkind remarks.

Amid the impoverished state we find ourselves in, we believe we do not deserve it, because we are simply going through tough times that will be over soon. We end up feeling sorry for ourselves.

Nonetheless, who amongst us has never received assistance from those benevolent creatures, from those altruistic angels who live among us and are always willing to help, without thinking twice? Who does not have one of those very close?

Generosity is an action that equates to charity, and both are virtues by excellence; they are innate gifts some people have ingrained in their hearts.

Those who are charitable, who try to understand others' needs in order to assist them, who do not seek to accumulate material goods solely for personal satisfaction, and help without exhibitionism, those are the truly generous beings—so rare among us.

These people are blessed; they have found the Path, they know the Truth, and they have learnt the value of Life.

20
WORK

From the outset, work has been a constant obligation in our lives, necessary as it is to our survival, our wellbeing, and our moral and intellectual development.

It is at work and during our interactions with our peers that we apply the precious lessons assimilated by means of examples presented to us during our childhood, through books we have had access to, or even from our own personal experiences.

It is so good to have a job, to have somewhere to go where we can spend our daily or nightly hours on something that can secure our home's subsistence and comfort and keep our minds busy, so they do not get lost in the shadows' indolence.

Working is also a means of contributing towards humanity's continued progress.

It does not matter what type of job we do, because all of them combined have a single value. Whether a job entails great responsibilities, upon which other lives depend, or whether it is a simple job, requiring little physical or mental effort, they are all important. This is a fact.

There are countless types of work, but we cannot always choose the one we would like, so we settle for what is available to us at the moment.

Often times, though, we end up doing a job we do not like, which gives us no gratification whatsoever, for an indefinite amount of time.

This may happen for lack of opportunities or even for a lack of determination to look for a more gratifying job we would be able to perform with greater joy.

We are consequently dissatisfied and frustrated at work and end up creating an environment filled with energies that are not healthy as a result of our bad mood and discontent. This may even contaminate our nearby peers, who may no longer enjoy having us among them.

On the other hand, there are those blessed ones who work with enthusiasm and dedication, always going above and beyond what is expected of them, turning work hours into an actual observation lab for displaying the positive skills they already possess and for sharing them among their workmates.

With this overt humanitarian feeling, these people end up spreading their positive energy to everyone or even inspiring some people to conduct a deep reflection about their own conduct, often sloppy, with regard to their job. The work may, then, unfold in a more gratifying and harmonic rhythm.

It is always good to keep in mind that personal problems should not be associated with those we will certainly have to face at work and vice versa. One thing has nothing to do with the other, and if we can dissociate them, we will certainly have more harmony and emotional balance in our lives.

We cannot forget that we must always spice up our duties and obligations with a pinch of love, this powerful feeling we all carry inside.

In doing so, we will certainly be able to turn the hours of anxiety at work into a more pleasant time. As a consequence, they will pass by a lot faster.

Imagine if we no longer had a job. Do we need this to actually happen so we can finally recognize the value of what we have lost? How can we face the challenges in our search for a new job?

Where should we even begin?

These questions may be avoided altogether as long as we fulfill our current duties with due diligence and respect.

In order to accomplish this, we must always do our best and go a little beyond what is required from our position. With that kind of positive attitude, we will certainly reap, in a near future, the gratifying fruits of our efforts in overcoming the obstacles presented to us by disturbed minds.

21
TIME

Countless people have already talked about or shared their personal opinions regarding time.

Many have even used this highly controversial topic as inspiration for their poetry, books, songs, lectures. There is always a lot to be said about time, because this treasured soul consoler allows the dust raised along our paths to slowly settle down and it carries us along—way further than our imaginations can reach.

There is a time for everything: a time to forget the ingratitude we have been a victim of, or a loved one who has abandoned us; a time to forget a distant land where we came into this world, which we had to get away from; and even a time to stop suffering for a loved one who has gone ahead on their journey to the other side of life.

Sometimes, when longing tugs at our heartstrings, it feels so good to go back in time and relive childhood moments, for example, when we relished such joy that did not even seem real because there were no worries or decisions to make.

We lived as if in a fairy tale; we were royalty living in candy castles, surrounded by dragons and knights to protect us. Everything was part of an innocent imagination and a sincere bond with dear friends.

Sometimes we want to hold on to time, to prevent it from passing by when a wave of fortunate events involves us, when everything is going as we wish and our days are free from any worries.

We may even feel a twinge of happiness in our hearts. We then implore for time to stand still, to not pass by, to not go away; but it does...

Other times, though, what we really wish is that time would fly by quickly, carrying away with it all of our grievances, anguish, and broken dreams. We then attempt to erase this time of horror and tragedy that comes into our lives once in a while.

In these instances, we ask ourselves why will this time never end? Why will this time not fly away quickly, as it does during fortunate moments? Instead, it drags on for a long while...

Time gradually transforms nature, enhances the landscape, generates more favorable conditions, enables discoveries of significant importance to humanity. Likewise, time takes on the task of placating feelings and emotions.

We are no longer the same people we were before; we have matured with time; we now act and think more carefully.

From now on, we make decisions with the confidence they have been well thought out; we look at someone else's mistakes with more understanding and we do not blame others with lightning speed like we used to do.

Time goes by and the valuable lessons pile on in our minds and in our hearts.

To embrace time is to live wisely, to enrich our knowledge, and to enjoy from life the best it has to offer.

Those who do not embrace time in order to become aware of the mistakes they have made and attempt to fix them, those who regret and get frustrated over unfulfilled goals, and even those who spend their whole lives in a state of idleness—they are like children who make mistakes during their lessons and need to repeat them until they reach the correct result.

We must put faith on time, this treasured friend we can always count on. Time only accommodates within us what must be saved or forgotten.

22
FRIENDSHIP

Friends, we all have many. But can we always count on them, especially during our hours of oppression and suffering? During those times when we do not know which path to take in our lives?

We certainly want to hear from our friends the words we do not dare say, which can give us the encouragement we need at the moment if they come from a friend.

You see, we want our friends to say the words we want to hear, and not words that might discourage us, even when we are wrong. That is because friends, for us, are those who think the same way we do and never contradict us.

Is this really what we mean by friendship? Are those our real friends?

Over the course of our existence, we get to know different types of people; we cultivate all sorts of friendships. Some of those friendships are sincere and genuine—those are priceless.

We are sometimes able to retain a treasured friend from childhood until life's laws of nature break us apart. Other times, we are only able to establish this type of friendship when we reach maturity. In some rare instances, we only find valuable friends at very sporadic stages of our journey through the paths of life.

It is such a rare jewel to have a friend like this, someone who cares about us, who values us for what we are and not for what we have.

A friend who sends us invaluable words of sincere friendship even when physically distant, because they know us and are aware of our weaknesses and possibilities.

Nonetheless, if we are also true friends to our friends, we shall respect the opinions they have to offer us, regardless of what they are—even if their advice is the opposite of what we hoped to hear.

The value of a friendship is measured by the sincere and mutual well wishes and affection one has for the other, always aiming solely at reciprocal happiness.

If there is something to be debated, this must be done in a harmonious environment until a solution and common agreement is reached.

A true friend is the one who will often tell us what we do not want to hear but need to in order to face whatever it is that is going on in our lives at the moment.

When we have a friendship like that, we must preserve it throughout our existence and even beyond...

We must, however, be alert so we do not make the huge mistake of turning our children into our friends, merely.

To them, we are mentors and educators, which goes beyond friendship. We are responsible for the goals they accomplish in their lives and for the kindness they manage to amass in their hearts.

Fortunate are those who can count on a true, genuine friendship in the hours of sorrow as well as in the moments of joy.

Sharing the joy is just as valuable as facing together painful challenges that life always has in store for us.

We must also never forget the greatest Friend we have, though many do not know Him yet.

He, who is always by our side, cheering for us to succeed, to win the battles against our inner sores...

That One True Friend who loves us unconditionally.

23
BANKRUPTCY

This is a delicate matter to discuss—especially among those who have had the misfortune of experiencing, at some point in their lives, an embarrassing situation such as bankruptcy.

It is so hard because one has not yet managed to forget the personal drama experienced, which has affected oneself deeply.

Bankruptcy is almost impossible to accept for some people, because they know the downfall and total loss may have been caused by an accounting error, a small mistake, or even neglect of duty. For those people, the scar will never heal.

On the other hand, there are people who can relive the event internally or even talk about it without resentment or the feeling of inferiority that often afflicts those who have failed—because they have been morally and psychologically strengthened as time went by.

They know they have been a victim of an unfortunate event that led them to drastic changes and new paths. They understand they need to keep going, though, to start over...

There are still some instances when bankruptcy is brought about by someone we used to trust completely, someone who had been our partner, working on the construction of a small fortress. Unfortunately, they may have become so helplessly thrilled by the consequent increase in wealth and status that each party ended up taking opposite paths, which they should never have ventured into.

These people, lured by the situation's luxuries and perks, end up carelessly destroying everything that had been built over several years of hard work, sacrifices, and obstacles overcome with great difficulty.

As a consequence, with such imprudent attitude they destroy a small empire that could have grown even more and become well established through the decades.

These people, unfortunately, will never get back on their feet; they cannot accept the consequences of their actions; they are unwilling to do it. They end their days constantly evoking the wealth they used to have and did not manage to preserve.

Most bankruptcy victims themselves would not be able to pinpoint exactly where the downfall began, or at which moment it became impossible to do anything that could have spared them from this financial tragedy.

The pain that follows bankruptcy is inestimable, because the person is forced to completely change the path of their lives, and their family's lives too, overnight...

Bankruptcy is a blow to the person's guts; it thus brings to the surface the worst feeling anyone can cultivate: pride.

In addition to losing everything they have built, bankrupt individuals are also compelled to give away whatever is left of their small fortune in order to preserve their reputation and be able to end up with nothing, as long as their honor is intact. This is a commendable choice that many opt for.

There are still those who, unable to bear the weight of such overwhelming sorrow and shame, decide to put an end to their own lives, leaving behind their families, completely helpless.

Finally, there are others who manage to get back on their feet and quickly rebuild a new life with good chances of prospering in a near future.

When we are still young or very little, we cannot understand what is going on, why we have to move to an unfamiliar place and leave behind those who are a part of our existence. It may seem strange, surreal to us.

We are taken away without too many explanations; some details surrounding our new situation may not even be disclosed to us. We go on, though, without protesting.

Deep inside our hearts, however, we will forever preserve our childhood's story, the first chapter in the book of our lives. A chapter that has been concluded but will always be treasured...

Any resentments? None. We were not the ones making the decisions at the time.

We had to simply obey and avoid asking too many questions so as not to cause any discomfort. We had to show respect and love for those who were our guardians and gave us the best they could at that time.

24
DREAMS

I was driving on a road that was totally foreign to me. Picturesque landscapes with different types of trees never before seen. It looked like a well-structured rural street, because you could see groups of animals quietly grazing at a distance, white picket fences surrounding portions of the land, and a few houses far away from each other.

Every once in a while, you could see small groves of blooming apple trees, filled with white flowers, which made the landscape that unveiled before my eyes seem indescribably and uniquely charming.

Everything was well manicured: the road, the white fences, the apple orchards, and the blue sky filled with white clouds. Everything was so beautiful; it was such a bliss to be able to appreciate so much beauty all at once.

I was driving a car that did not seem familiar to me while enjoying the landscape ahead when the car's engine started making a strange sound and suddenly gave warning signs it was going to fail. I barely had enough time to move the car to the shoulder.

"And now what?" I thought to myself. What could I possibly do? I was all alone, and I had no idea where I was. I remembered I had just passed by a house that was not too far behind. Maybe

I could walk there and have someone let me use their phone to ask for help.

That is what I did. I locked the car and walked back along the shoulder, hoping that maybe another car would come in the opposite direction and help me out.

I finally arrived in front of the house I had seen and not a single car had passed by me. I still had no idea what awaited me or what I would find there.

In front of the door of this small and cozy home, I became pensive, hesitant. But what else could I do if not to take a chance? That is exactly what I did. I rang the doorbell and waited.

It was such a surprise for me when an older man greeted me warmly and promptly asked how he could help.

I could not recognize his face, I could not make up his features, but I felt like I could trust him, because his voice was tender and kind.

This made me feel safe, though I could not immediately understand the reason for so much kindness on his part or for so much trust from me.

After I explained what had happened, he promptly offered to help with whatever I needed, all the while sharing small details about his life with me, to make sure I was comfortable. Everything was so strange...

He said his son was a mechanic in his free time and he would help me fix the issue with my car in a flash. He then led me to the back of the house, where his son was working. I followed him in awe—"How can he be so kind to someone he has never seen before when he cannot be sure I am telling the truth, treating me as if we had known each other for years?"

It was quite a surprise for me when I got to the other side of the house. What I saw fascinated me. A huge plot of land, which I figured was his property, which extended from one extreme to the other. It was completely covered by all types of vegetables and legumes you can imagine. Rows and rows of all varieties and colors, surrounded by blooming apple trees that perfectly contoured the giant vegetable garden, the largest one I had ever seen.

The diversity of colors in the rows, neatly separated by small ditches everywhere you walked, was a feast for the eyes. Everything was well taken care of. So neat, in fact, it looked more like a Bob Ross[4] painting.

The terrain had a slight drop right in the middle. There was someone there, bent down and completely distracted by whatever he was doing, because he did not notice our presence.

The old man by my side called out his name, and as soon as he heard his dad's voice, he got up, a little curious, and started walking towards us.

As he approached, I started to see him better. Stunned, I could not believe my eyes…

That is when I woke up!

What is a dream? Why do we dream? What do our dreams mean? Who can possibly explain our dreams? And why is it that people often cannot remember what they have dreamt about?

When we sleep, our body rests, because we are made of organic matter and we need to recharge our batteries, our physical and mental fuel, so we can continue working on whatever it is we need to do each day.

Everyone needs some rest. But our soul, our essence, does it also require rest?

Maybe someday science will be able to answer these questions we all mull over, especially children. They also look for answers.

Let us wait for new scientific developments, which progress by leaps and bounds in an effort to figure out the enigmas we still cannot comprehend.

Meanwhile, let us continue to dream, without worrying so much about what cannot yet be explained.

To dream, we do not need to be sleeping, though. Many of us dream about the future, for example, about what we may still accomplish one day.

---

[4] Bob Ross was an American painter who lived from 1942 to 1995. He was also an art instructor, the creator and presenter of the Joy of Painting TV show from 1983 to 1994. Today, he is posthumously considered an Internet celebrity.

It is important not to live solely on dreams, however. We must hope they will come true and, meanwhile, do whatever we can to make it happen. We cannot simply stand by and wait for them to come true; we must put up a fight—without becoming impatient or even discouraged, because our dreams shall come true at the right time.

To believe in our dreams and particularly in ourselves is to live the present in the best possible way, taking advantage of the opportunities that come up.

We must also learn from our mistakes, because they are precious lessons we need in order to finally achieve our ultimate accomplishment.

The obstacles along the way are there to test our persistence in making sure our own wishes and efforts prevail so we can fulfill our goals, our dreams.

How many of us have already managed to make at least one of our dreams come true?

25
COURAGE

A good deal of courage is required in order to go through nearly a whole existence, filled with constant arduous, daunting, and often humiliating struggles, brimming with farewells, sacrifices, and new beginnings.

An immense mental effort, a firm commitment, and lots of determination, among other things, have been necessary in order to overcome some phobias that used to terrorize us.

Nonetheless, the boldness to challenge the obstacles ahead have spoken louder within us and we have then forged ahead, facing our fears and uncertainties.

Gradually, we have gained the necessary courage to reach our goals.

And we have then realized we have been brave warriors, and each small victory accomplished has served as the impetus, the fuel, the push we needed not to retreat or wither so we could get to where we currently are.

The show of life must go on with its performance, does it not? Despite the bitter failures we have experienced, which certainly have been many, we have not lost our strength; we have not cowered.

It is rewarding to know that by the end of this journey, we will be able to depart knowing we have done at least some good and precious deeds. And to realize that the final stage of one's existence has been filled with lessons, overcome deserts, and personal renovation—all of this because we did not lack the courage to keep moving on.

Yes, we need great inner strength to live, to face the risks, perils, and crossroads ahead without losing control or falling into despair.

This is especially the case when we are all alone in this struggle and must keep going even when life surprises us with occasional setbacks.

We therefore need a great deal of courage to realize how puny and insignificant we are compared to outer space, which sits right above us and is still unknown to us.

We need courage, indeed, to uncover what lies within us, which we still do not know. This is our greatest challenge.

We also need the humility to accept the imperfections we have, like everyone else, which need to be corrected, rectified.

Finally, we need to be humble and tolerant in our interactions with one another. In order to accomplish this, courage is also necessary.

This is one of the virtues we must cultivate: courage. It may be the most challenging one, because how can we possibly evolve morally, physically, and intellectually without it?

How can we reach our goals if we need to fight for them? What if we lack the courage? How would we then be able to encourage our loved ones, our friends, and close companions who are facing situations way more dire than us without becoming distressed or falling into despair?

How can we keep up our faith, the source of our spiritual support, or even persevere on the path we have chosen to follow, knowing the shadows of our inferior passions will try to discourage us?

We therefore need a lot of courage indeed, for everything we decide to do—particularly to change what needs to be changed within us.

Let us keep forging ahead, then—without fear, without hesitation, and without slowing down. We will not lack the courage, especially not when we must testify as to what we have made of our lives.

26
HATE

"I hate you!"

What an obnoxious expression for someone to hear. It emanates such a negative and sinister energy that originates from the person who carries this feeling inside.

Hate is one of those passions we still cultivate within due to ignorance, maybe. It slowly erodes our bodies and souls without us realizing it. Each and all negative feelings trigger many incurable diseases, which humanity still ignores.

Therefore, the longer we take to fight off this destructive feeling we allow to lodge within our hearts, the more this poison deteriorates our most beautiful feelings and we become ungrateful children of the One who has created us with pure love.

Yes, hate is the flipside of love; it dilutes love. Hate is the most dreadful among all our other passions because those who carry hate in their hearts carry within a bomb of great yet invisible destructive power.

The person who carries hate towards someone, whomever it may be, does not realize that the first person affected by this hate is its carrier; only then may this hate reach others.

This insane passion is our invisible enemy. It is just like a virus, which is detrimental to our health even though we cannot see it, unless we use powerful microscopes. Hate affects us in the same way—silently. And it gradually creates an internal disorder, with grim consequences we only realize a lot later.

It also progressively tarnishes our souls, involving them with a deep, dark color, like the shadow of a great sorrow.

Hate gives rise to all of that in those who allow themselves to become involved by this despicable feeling. It also causes considerable heartbreak to those who love them and see this destructive passion take over them, because they do not yet realize the consequences of this malady they carry inside.

How can we help them, free them from this malevolent passion, then? What might have happened that allowed this hate to lodge inside them?

It may have been a betrayal, a slander, a major heartbreak, a touch of envy, a humiliating event. Whatever happened that has led us to hate, we need to revert this feeling; we must not let it escalate or even last long.

Now we know the malevolent effects of hate, this heinous passion that is so detrimental to our health because it leaves sequelae of great sorrow within us. And we must resist it.

We must appease our feelings and steadily settle our hearts, because it would not be prudent to allow this hate we feel for someone to become stronger than the love we feel for ourselves.

This will not be an easy task to tackle, but it is necessary.

We can start by gradually transforming our hate into anger; after a while, we may substitute our anger for disappointment or frustration; a little while later, we shall be able to feel only heartbreak; and so on.

We cannot stop hating immediately, because we have not yet reached this level of emotional evolution; but if we already know ourselves well enough, then we must certainly aspire to it.

And what is an aspiration? Would it possibly be the tool we have on hand, which we must use for our own benefit?

27
RESPONSIBILITY

Since early on in our lives, from a very young age, responsibility has summoned us to be accountable for our duties. This responsibility lasts throughout most of our existence.

It does not end until we are already bent over by the weight of the years accumulated over our shoulders and our steps have become heavy, due to the burden of all the obligations we have undertaken throughout this long journey, filled with useful lessons and somewhat fulfilled duties.

These obligations gradually become a burden, which is sometimes very hard to balance. This is particularly the case when we are still teenagers, who have just left behind childhood games and porcelain dolls.

Still immature, we do not clearly comprehend that we must always be in control of our actions and choices when facing the various circumstances we may have to confront in life.

We must be in control at all times so we do not have to prematurely and, without sufficient knowledge, decide which path to take. Thus, we avoid unnecessary suffering to ourselves and to that small being that depends upon us.

Even after years in open captivity, surrounded by uncertainty regarding our future, we again need to make choices. Once again life imposes responsibilities upon us, because the safety of our loved ones will depend upon what we decide to make of ourselves.

This is so even if we do not yet realize that our decisions—right or wrong—will affect our loved ones.

Even when, unexpectedly, our main goal becomes a reality; or when we finally decide to cross the boundaries of our limitations, do something never before dreamt. Even if doubts come up and grow within us when the time comes to take the most pungent and painful decision of our lives, compared to all our previous ones.

This is when duty calls us, once again, to be responsible for choosing the path we shall take from then on.

Even when we are sure this will bring us much sorrow, particularly an indescribable longing for the loved ones who are absent, though the aim will always be a future with more and better opportunities for all.

We now know that in order to reach our highest ideals, we must pay a price. We will have to sacrifice something, because we do not get anything unless something else is taken away from us first.

But we also learn that the more we give ourselves away, the more we will certainly get in return.

We must therefore be aware that in order for this to happen, countless woes and sorrows will certainly strike us.

This may be due to our ignorance regarding the laws of good living, which we should have tried to learn, follow, and respect from the very beginning.

It may also be a result of our unwillingness to accept our mistakes and vulnerabilities.

Because it is still very hard for us, human beings, to take responsibility for the decisions we have made, for our past actions that did not work out, for our failures and defeats.

We then run away from our commitment before our conscience and blame our fate, nature, bad luck for it, or someone else; anything but the one who is really responsible: "ourselves!"

28
SHORTAGE

In the last two centuries, our planet may have experienced the greatest development that humanity has ever witnessed. Across all different sectors, from medicine to technology, labor, arts, and research. In other words, we have taken a major step ahead.

There have been countless discoveries; we have news of numerous studies and experiments conducted around the globe, which have significantly contributed to making our lives easier and keeping us closer to one another, even when we are far apart.

Certainly, from now on our challenges and our goals will be even more ambitious. We shall soon cross boundaries that might have seemed impossible to surmount earlier. Who can say how far we will reach with so many perspectives in sight?

Unfortunately, and despite all of this evolution, there are still all sorts of shortages in our daily lives. The deprivation that countless creatures still experience is devastating.

While many people take for granted the abundance they experience, many others can barely stand due to hunger, thirst, and the lack of a roof over their head where they can find shelter.

We see an abundance of shortages everywhere, which we have not yet been able to tackle. Or maybe we are not giving this problem the importance it urgently demands.

We often have our tables laden with food and we are not even grateful for it, while our neighbor does not even have a piece of bread to stave off the hunger.

This inequality is still gargantuan on our planet, which is still filled with constant struggles and challenges.

What can we say of those people who face major trials when they are unable to seek a job that might ensure their livelihood because of their maternal duties and cannot count on anyone to help them?

And sadly, at the end of the day, with an almost completely empty stomach, they have to say to their loved ones: "Sleep, my dear, because slumber is nurturing."

How many people are currently experiencing such a rough reality?

We also witness everywhere the affection shortage take over people, who are still apprentices of the way and inexperienced, so they allow themselves to fall into despair for lacking what nurtures the deepest part of our souls: affection, understanding, guidance, and love.

These feelings are indispensable in order to maintain our emotional balance.

These same creatures often cannot stand the burden of so much pain and are led by the terrible desire to take their own lives in a desperate and insane attempt to escape their own reality.

Even with so many possibilities ahead, so many ingenious minds, so many breakthroughs and aspirations, we still have a major issue, and it is up to all of us to tackle, overcome, and eradicate it.

That is, if we indeed want to find safety and peace within our hearts. This will only become a reality, though, when there is no longer one single soul in need of something in the planet.

Many people might then ask, How can this be possible if we hardly have the means for anything? Governing authorities detain the power in their hands and are the mighty ones on Earth; this job is up to them.

Using an old fable I have heard many years ago as an example, the simple answer resides in our conscience:

"In a large, faraway forest, a frightening fire burned everything one could imagine, devastating the green vegetation and leaving the animals terrified. Amid an unhinged rat race, all the forest creatures tried to escape, desperately running away. Mammals, reptiles, birds, all of them sought refuge outside the burning and almost completely destroyed forest. An elephant that was running past a water source did not contain his surprise and stopped to observe a peculiar scene:

A hummingbird was flying away from the spring, where it had filled its beak with water, and quickly flew towards the forest fire. It dropped the water and hurriedly came back to do it all over again.

The elephant then asked him, irascible: "Are you crazy? Do you think you alone can put out the fire? Run away, save yourself."

The small bird, nevertheless, continued working and replied: "I know I am very small and cannot do much, but I am doing MY PART!"

29
RELATIONSHIPS

Some of the basic principles in a couple's relationship for it to last are, without any doubt, honesty and then trust. This is the case in a romantic relationship, in a friendship, in work interactions, and even among relatives.

Honesty is indispensable; it must function as the foundation and basis for any relationship so there is harmony and affectionate candor between the two people who live under the same roof or spend a great deal of their time together.

We frequently see relationships that come to an end after a really small amount of time spent together. What is worse, most of the times one of the parties ends up seriously hurt.

The other party, on the contrary, continues on their path without any weight in their conscience, having quickly forgotten what has been left behind, moving on in new directions or new adventures.

In other instances, there are more violent cases, where everything seems fine in the beginning but end up in major disagreements, unfortunately. This may be due to all sorts of incompatibility, which intensify as time goes by. Many of these cases have tragic endings, involving great sorrow.

Nevertheless, there are also happy relationships where people fall in love and spend the rest of their lives together, perfectly united and fulfilled by all the unforgettable achievements and events, living together in great harmony and happiness as they overcome together all the challenges that may come up.

There are so many different circumstances we can witness in relationships we are familiar with—each with their own stories and experiences accumulated through the years these couples have spent living together.

It is important to remember there must be honesty from the very beginning of any relationship. We must always be open and candid, dialoguing and explaining what is going on within us—even when we feel that we lack the courage to tell our dear partner what is bothering us, what we would like to accomplish together, and particularly when the love dwindles and practically disappears.

This way, if the relationship must end, it will not be amid a battle of greedy and selfish feelings but in a considerate and friendly environment, respected by both parties—especially if there are little ones involved.

When there is honesty, trust goes hand in hand and will not allow jealousy, which causes so much discomfort and emotional pain, to present itself in the relationship.

If we allow our inferior passions to expand so much as to surpass our most sublime virtues, a relationship will become impossible. No relationship can survive in an environment like this, based on outright disagreement and daily conflicts, and withstand the storms it must have already faced and the other storms still to come—which shall be even more severe than the previous ones.

The years spent amid several relationships have led me to the realization that we must preserve our dignity as apprentices of the path, which we still are. We must curb our unexpected impulses, our outbursts of anger, and our hurt pride—which always stand out in these circumstances.

It is primarily in these moments of affective stupor that life presents us with an opportunity to experience the challenge of conquering ourselves.

This is an opportunity to conquer and tame our inferior instincts, which are still very primitive and beastly.

30
AGING

...And our old age slowly approaches until, one day, it finally reaches us.

Then our hair is not as silky, smooth, or shiny as before and they turn silver.

Our appearance starts to gradually decay due to sagging skin and the now quite visible wrinkles, which have slowly become deeper with time—maybe due to the storms faced during our unfortunate days.

Our strength has declined as the years went by. We no longer have the same stamina we once did, when we could do many things at the same time without getting tired—which now happens quickly and more intensely.

It is true, old age does not spare anyone; we will all have to face it, sooner or later. For many of us, though, this is terrifying or even cruel.

These people will try anything. They will spend all the material resources they have and resort to all the cosmetic options available just to avoid aging; just so they do not have to face this so soon.

They live in a constant battle against the dreaded aging process, which often afflicts them prematurely, because they did not know any better during their golden years and did not abstain from vices and bad habits that go against our physical nature and accelerate aging. They then try to avert it at all costs, as if it were a contagious illness.

What is old age, though? What does it mean to become a senior citizen? Or even to "be over the hill," as many people say?

Would it mean that we no longer have the same appearance, energy, and vitality we had before? Or that we have become someone who can no longer be counted or depended on?

How about all the things we have compiled within us—everything we have learnt so far, during our "years by the window"?

The virtues we have developed by going through the numerous pains and sorrows we have experienced in life; the happy moments that remain engraved in our memories as if printed in a beloved book, even if there are not too many of those.

All the good we have done to those who have shared our journey until now, even if it was not as much as we should have done. At least we have done it all gladly.

All these things we carry inside should be enough reason to embrace old age. It should be enough to know that others will be able to benefit from our deeds, and therefore, their rough climbing to the top of the Sacred Mountain will be a little easier, empowered by additional wisdom and better judgment gained from us.

Oh, my! The years we have spent during our beauty and youth days do not seem that long ago; we can still recall what we have left behind, the happy moments among our loved ones, which we keep safe within our hearts. These are precious memories, necessary to make us feel, deep inside, that we are still young and that our chronological age does not intimidate us.

Also, we cannot ignore that we once were like pretty flower buds of singular beauty. In those days, dreams about our future—filled with great deeds and sprinkled with joy—nurtured our days and nights.

We were indeed fragrant, delicate buds in bright tones, and that was enough at the time to encourage us to pursue our aspirations and our most daring reveries, facing the challenges that came up ahead of us.

Then, one day, this bud opened up and the flower that now seems tired and feeble still resonates a strange, different, and inexplicable energy, unlike anything we have ever known.

We must not grieve for the fact that our appearance is no longer the same or because we do not recognize this weird creature we now see when we look into the mirror—a creature that looks back at us with curiosity and surprise.

We need not grieve, because we can now count on this renewed interior strength that has settled within our hearts.

Old age, therefore, must not terrify or intimidate us. We will once again overcome this new, additional obstacle that life has presented to us with wisdom.

We will age with kindness and understanding towards our limitations and not become grumpy and idle old people. We will work until we really have no more strength left, so we do not become a heavy burden and "persona non grata" to those around us.

We will be contented with the youth of those around us without feeling envy and will not recriminate them for actions we know they will regret one day. We must remember that we have also made bad choices in the past.

Let us then welcome the age of maturity and let us hope our freedom of choice will be respected, always.

And let us hope the upcoming years may still bring us new experiences, challenges, and clashes with our own imperfections, which are still plentiful.

We will then learn, even in our final moments, because we cannot waste the time that has been entrusted to us and for which we will be accountable one day.

31
IF...

If I knew, in the beginning, what I now know...

Oh, dear soul, I would have done many things differently so the sorrow I carry with me from past mistakes would never, ever affect me.

If I had been stronger and more determined...

Oh, dear soul, I would not have allowed any pain to afflict you, as a child. I would have defended you with my maternal claws so the scars you bear today would never have blemished such a selfless being. Though you have now learnt to ignore them, after much struggle.

If I knew yesterday what I know today...

Oh, dear soul, I would have guided you, from a young age, towards this path of light you showed me yourself one day, which I trail today; a path that leads us to understand our misfortunes. I would then be able to get rid of dreadful events that have scarred you in the early days of your existence.

If I knew yesterday what I know today...

Oh, dear soul, I would talk to you from an early age, and I would teach you how to trust your own inner greatness, and I would defend you from the traps set by the greedy and ruthless wolves, by those who do not realize the virtues we must cultivate and instead fixate themselves on despicable passions from unbalanced souls.

If I knew yesterday what I know today...

Oh, dear soul, if I knew the secrets and mysteries hidden in the crossroads along the paths of our existence, I would have prepared myself better to tread them with you, and I would have done for you a lot more than you needed me to.

If I knew yesterday what I know today...

Oh, dear soul...

If I have a new opportunity...

Oh, dear soul...

32
About the Author

Selma Denmark was born in Brazil on December 21, 1952, in a small town in the state of São Paulo called Aguaí, where she spent a happy childhood among relatives and dear friends.

She got married in 1971, when she was still a teenager, and moved to the greater metropolitan area of the city of São Paulo. She had four children: Rodrigo, Mirna Maria, Nívia Maria, and Mateus.

In 1982 she divorced and went back to her hometown, where she lived with her children. At the time, she held three different jobs, one of which was at a local newspaper called *O IMPARCIAL*, an opportunity presented to her by the editor-in-chief. Even though she did not hold a degree in journalism, because she had always cultivated the habit of writing, she authored some interesting articles and was responsible for two pages in the newspaper.

She then became quite popular in town for the articles she wrote for the newspaper, such as: Gossip Column, Interviews, Stories Told by the People, and Dreams of my Dreams. This last one ended up turning into her first book, published in 1985.

In 1989 she moved to the United States of America and gradually got used to the country's customs and lifestyle.

As time went by, she grew fond of the country, started to study English, got a job in a diner, and kept moving ahead, always working to support her children, who had stayed behind in Brazil, in the care of their grandmother.

Today, divorced a second time, she lives in Milton, New York. Her children have gotten married and given her eight grandchildren: Felipe, Alyssa Maria, Helena, Caio Francisco, Ana Laura, Maria Luiza, Lucas José, and Karys Marie.

After treading such a long journey, which has enabled her to develop a certain degree of emotional stability and to realize we all need to get to know ourselves better in order to be able to face whatever awaits us each day, she decided to write her second book.

This time, it is based on her own reality. The book aims to encourage her dear readers not to give in to total despondency when they have to face barriers of sorrow that may eventually come up along the path they are trailing. Because that is how it is: if we cannot take them down, we can at least go around them. In other words, there is always something we can do, ALWAYS!

CPSIA information can be obtained
at www.ICGtesting.com
Printed in the USA
LVHW050835200122
708837LV00011B/747

9 781638 673279